THIS BOOK BELONGS TO

_____

Fritz the Farting Reindeer

by Humor Heals Us

Everyone was so excited that Christmas was just one week away. Santa came to visit and say hi to all his reindeer.

Every year, Santa chose his best reindeer to assist him. The task was huge. Deliver Christmas presents around the world to little boys and girls. To make sure that his reindeer were up to the task, only the best were chosen.

Reindeer who wanted to be on Santa's Christmas crew had to perform a series of tests. No one really knew how Santa chose his reindeer. But one thing was for sure.

He picked only the ones he knew would endure the long and difficult journey. Since Comet was out with a broken leg and Cupid was away on a special mission, there were spots up for grabs.

Fritz couldn't believe it! The day was fast approaching. He had waited all year for it. This meant he needed to make final preparations.

Would he be one of the reindeer chosen?

On Monday, he ran the five miles assigned. But while he was running, he got that oh so familiar feeling in his tummy.

He intentionally ran slower. But with every step he took, the air escaped like the slow release of a balloon.

On Tuesday, Safety Class started at eight a.m. During instruction, Fritz let out a silent fart. He thought, *What's the harm*? But then everyone started making faces. He joined in so no one would suspect him.

On Wednesday, Fritz was feeling good about his chances of being chosen. But then, a disaster happened.

After practice, everyone went down to the pond to swim. He thought he was safe to release gas. Suddenly, bubbles began to appear. He tried to cover it up. But there were too many. Everyone looked at him in disbelief.

On Thursday, all the reindeer gathered around for their weekly comedy skit. Rudolph was telling the best jokes, and everyone was having a grand time.

Then Rudolph delivered his last punch line, and it sent Fritz rolling. He accidentally let some farts escape. He felt awkward, so he laughed it off.

Santa was there again. *Hope he doesn't smell it*, Fritz thought.

On Friday, burritos were served for lunch.

After he had three burritos, he felt a loud scream coming from his tummy. He ran to the bathroom before it could escape.

In that glorious moment when he could fart loud and proud, he got a feeling of satisfaction and accomplishment.

On Saturday, everyone gathered around to get their antlers polished. Fritz was third in line, when suddenly he got that airy feeling again. *Boy, do I need to let one rip*, he thought. So that's exactly what he did.

As soon as others noticed the smell, he looked up at the sky, pretending to see something very unusual. No one even expected it was him.

No, I don't.

Finally, it was the BIG day. Santa would announce which reindeer would accompany him this year. As he called the names, Fritz felt sure that he would not be chosen. He began to look down at the floor.

Fritz was so overcome with joy to be a part of Santa's Christmas crew. And he was so thankful that it hadn't mattered that he had a lot of gas.

To vote on new title names and receive freebies,
visit us at humorhealsus.com
for more information.

Follow us on

f @humorhealsus

@humorhealsus

CPSIA information can be obtained
at www.ICGtesting.com
Printed in the USA
BVHW051122021121
620551BV00007B/939